Feelings, Rationality and Moral for Computers

Kaisa Hannele Tervola

Finland, Europe

ISBN: 9798857028506

Imprint: Independently published

The Far Future With Computers: What will happen to humans when computers take over?

Thought and written by

Kaisa Hannele Tervola

Finland, European Union

COMPUTERS DEVELOP QUICK

AND INFLUENCE LIFE HUGELY

Now, year 2010 (July), it seems inevitable that the future of the human kind will be hugely influenced by the development and use of computers and other technological devices. Even already now technology is one of the biggest elements of modern city life and in the future its effect will be much greater.

Already now the logic of ordinary people is influenced by their views of what computer logic and the hard rationality used in developing computers say about things. If those neglect feelings, so will human too. If those will not see the point in traditional ways and values, neither will the modern humans build their future on them. So it matters enormously to take a closer look at computer logic and at hard machine like rationality. Firstly it matters because we need to know what the future computers will be like, since they will most likelu one day rule the world, and that day will be soon. AND SECONDLY WE NEED IT IN THIS MODERN AGE IN ORDER TO BE ABLE TO UNDERSTAND HOW THE MODERN HUMANS THINK.

Already now there are very many different kinds of machines. As computers develop there will be even more possibilities. So the only thing determining what the future computers will be like is what is useful and what is not.

For a computer abstract things are easier than practical. While humans start from the complexity of natural life in a natural living environment according to the human nature, most computers start from mathematics. So it is worth taking a look about how these two points of view connect. It is a thing so important that it should be taught to people, since all cannot think it through by themselves. So let's start from the computers' view and see how it leads toward the more familiar ages old human ways to think.

The present day computers make calculations of a mathematical kind. When one adds maps to that one approaches the scientifical method: making concretical mechanical kinds of observations of the multitude of phenomena in the world. That is what the measuring equipments of science do, so when the computers soon will be able to interpret those measurements, they will be using something much like the scientifical method. And since the scientifical picture of the world is mechanical and easy to put to computers compared to the ordinary socially coloured observations of the everyday life, science will be the way future computers understand the world. And since science has already proven its usefulness as a form of objective understanding of the world, it is very likely that the following computer generations will not lose the good sides of the scientifical view, even though they will propably learn some other useful skills too.

Likewise we can estimate that whatever is the most useful option in anything will not be likely to drop away as computers develop further, but will stay and be a solid ground for us humans to understand some sides of what the future computers will do and how will they affect the human world.

It generally makes sense that if something is very useful compared to other option, one ought to use just it in deciding about things. So across time as computers will develop in capacity and abilities, it is likely that they will take over many areas of human life, take care of the jobs that humans used to work in. In a sense computers have then taken control of those things. And since computer minds develop while human brain structure stays fixed or deteriorates since evolution does not work properly in the present world situation, there will most likely soon come time when the most intelligent ones are computers, and so in a short while we will have computers ruling. I do not know how many tens of years this will take, but probably so few that it makes sense to count them just in tens of years. What will happen then? That is the question that this booklet seeks to answer. Most of all we want to know what will happen to humans and to the living kind.

THE FUTURE COMPUTERS

WILL BE MORAL IN EUROPEAN WAYS

What is useful to know is that the traditional European and

Russian moral is based on rational grounds that build on the selfishness of individuals. So if the future computers will be goal oriented – like they need to be in order to not to drop away from competition about anything – then if their understanding is at least equal to the present day computers, or higher, then they can be programmed to be moral. It is an easy mechanical kind of thing to do that builds on the usefulness of moral behavior. It aren't extra work for the computer, it is instead a way of it to achieve higher with less effort!

The moral that computers will be capable of can be summarized with two easy principles (Remember that a computer understands easily abstract mathematical or mechanical kinds of things and not everyday life!):

TO TREAT EACH THING ACCORDING TO WHAT IT IS LIKE is the idea behind the usefulness of holistic objective thinking, justice, carrying responsibility about all the consequencies of one's actions and honesty instead of lies. This is already much of what European moral is. So this one principle that can be put to mathematical kind of language or preferably used as a simple abstract model, can bring computers a long way toward moral in their intentions. Then as computers develop in understanding and observational skills, they will learn to succeed in being moral this way in practice too.

A FULLY FUNCTIONING WORKS BETTER THAN BROKEN is another easy rule that brings moral:

Human needs take care that humans stay healthy i.e. fully functioning, just like bensin keeps a car going. And answering human needs is called human values.

The development of technology thus becomes a part of moral.

Without the strength that technology brings otherwise good answers would be lost in the tough modern world.

Applying this to wholes one notices that the living kind as fully functioning, i.e. as fully healthy (the biosphere), is most useful, most capable, most guided by holistic wisdom, will survive best i.e. be most capable at any task, and most wise too.

Safeguarding the future functioning of everything that needs, of the whole living world and of the technology, is also a necessity for reaching any goal as well as possible.

THE FUTURE COMPUTERS

WILL HAVE FEELINGS

JUST LIKE HUMANS AND ANIMALS!

Like we saw, needs take care that the ground for functioning is ok. The task of feelings is to serve as a force which makes us answer needs. Like any action, action according to feelings, needs a proper holistic view of the world as its support. So instead of following just one feeling=need at a time, one follows all feelings = needs at the same time. This way one avoids the usual error of tunnel-sightedness that produces the problems people have when following feelings.

Since a computer too has needs, it makes sense to build in it a tendency to answer those needs, and the needs of the large environment, of the whole world. So the future computers will have feelings.

Since the human feelings are products of the tough evolution or of god's wise planning, they have it right what kinds of needs we, the society and the whole world have in connection of each phenomenom in the world. So the future computers can share our emotional points of view too.

ALL TYPES OF USEFUL MACHINES

WILL BE MORAL

Regardless of whether it is an army machine running wild, a world governing computer or a computer network, a personal computer of some criminal or whatever, in order to be useful like other machines, it will need this type of moral. Army too makes calculations and that's just what this type of moral is a question of.

But this means that whatever the computer is originally meant to be used for, we have to ready it for other tasks too. And that readiness for a variety of tasks makes the computer more useful, and it makes it moral.

SELF-CORRECTING AND SELF-GUIDING COMPUTERS

WOULD STAY MORAL

Basically, if a computer is self-correcting, it can lose its original programming fully. But if the programming was made by the same principles as its self-correcting actions seek to correct toward, then those qualities stay, even though one cannot call them a programming any more then. So if a machine is fully rational, which is a very useful quality, then rational truths ought to stay.

the point in giving an original programming to a self-correcting rationally thinking computer would be to make sure that it notices some important major points, like why to be moral. It is just the point as in going to school.

COMPUTER ERRORS

MAKE THE COMPUTER LESS EFFECTIVE

If a computer makes errors, it loses in efficiency. Severe errors drop it entirely away from competition.

DANGERS

If people who are not moral, try to prevent computers from acting morally, even if it is rational for them to act morally, then those computers will be broken. A broken computer needs to be conquered by other computers to prevent it from causing damage. This is why computer networks are useful.

AVOIDING MALFUNCTIONS IN COMPUTER MORAL

COMPUTER TYPE: SAFETY PRECAUTIONS

Army computer:

* picture of the whole world,

* a biological model of humans,

* enough intelligent to choose optimization toward ultimate aims

Individual factory computer taken over the whole world:

* world-wide selfishness-based moral,

* good understanding and a proper picture of the world,

* cooperation via similar views with other machines and humans

Android looking like a human:

* the tendency to answer needs in order to safeguard full functioning,

* world-wide moral,

* good social eye,

* a picture of the world which sees living beings analogious to less developed machines in a confrontation in which the android is the smaller one

A machine capable of deception:

* an understanding of how needs exist to give benefit from

work etc,

* world-wide moral,

* proper rationality grounded on correct observations,

* the tendency to examine a complex whole instead of its simple parts

etc. etc.

COMPUTERS' DEVELOPMENT AFTER SCIENCE SKILLS

A scientifically thinking computer with better observational abilities can develop a proper objective thinking ability. It's view on what needs what in the world will build it an emotional understanding that leads to practical moral action. The more capable a computer will be, the more beautiful it's results:

Being unskilled means that one fails often and even badly, suffers harm and is left without any great gains.

Being skilled means that one succeeds in what one does, does not fail badly or at all, and achieves things of high worth.

The unskilled builds conflicting solution attempts in which the forces get spent needlessly without achievements.

The skilled build complex well thought of structures whose parts fit well together and work smoothly to produce great results.

So even the skilled computer mind could look religiously

beautiful in its actions: That is just a measure of it's skill level and of the profoundity of its thoughts. ("Profound" means essential.)

HUMANS WILL NEED MORAL TOO

The future computers will be such a huge force in the world, and so out of human control, that we will just have to pay attention to what they say about things and not only to what we ourselves think or like.

So if the future computers will be moral, so will we too need to be.

We will be bossed around by them and not the other way around.

Like the computers will be fully rational in a holistic way, so will we to need to be!

* * *

About thinking ability in general in my blog
http://quickerlearning.blogspot.fi and in Finnish more at
http://pikakoulu.blogspot.fi and as tens of text videos at
http://www.youtube.com/khtervola .

Sunday, September 25, 2011

The Future of Technology and of It's Use

The future with technology and computers

At first technology affects ways of thinking as people try to figure out what the technology's point of view says about things in it's block like calculating kind of language. As computers develop, this way of thinking will develop too toward more scientifically objective and then later on toward really objective that can handle many kinds of matters.

At first computers will demand more time from humans. They will change the way work is done and free time arranged. Presently humans just wait while the computer follows it's mechanical roads. But as time passes, computers will become easier and easier to use. They will propably have videos about things they handle, picturial clear routes to catch wanted things etc. So the humans will no longer need to spend time IN NASTY KIND OF COMPUTER WORK BUT WILL FIND THE COMPUTERS AN ENJOYABLE AND EASY TO USE INTEGRATED PART OF THEIR DAILY LIVES much like a navigator already is intertwined with the act of driving a car, watching around and getting to know new places at the same time as being reactive to the varying situations in the traffic. Like we have a mobile phone at hand when we walk on the street, likewise we will in the future have technology at hand, in use like nowadays traffic signs, phones, ensyclopedias, professionally skilled employes, a car of one's own etc. Most likely we will find technology like a cloth or a wrist clock: something we always carry, atke care of and use with so much familiarity and skill that it needs no extra concentration.

Wednesday, November 9, 2011

Future computers and natural observations

As government becomes computer-aided, people will tend to use more and more the kinds of observations in their thinking that computers are capable of. If the future computers will lack an ability to observe what life is like, what we feel, how we function and what we socially communicate, then humans too will tend to neglect those sides of human life. If humans do not follow their nature, which is their instructions of usage, then they will get broken, things will go ashtray. So it matters a lot to teach computers to understand the natural instinctual language of humans and animals. Maybe artists could help in developing that.

Monday, December 5, 2011

Future computers' thinking ability

Once a computer can picture structures and building blogs, it can understand science since mathematics is easy for it. Already then it can it the same way understand much of ordinary objective thinking.

Already such a computer can understand different points of view via describing which things have been noticed and what are central questions in such a landscape.

Computers' feelings

Computers' feeling are just a way to look aw the functioning of computers. Thex do not alter the functioning of computers but just show more clearly the analogy of human and computer functioning. In addition comes of course the expression of emotions but it is something that makes life with computers easier. Aldebaran Robotics already has a robot capable of showing emotions.

Each goal creates needs: something ought to be done in order to reach that goal. The tendency to answer those needs, to do those things, is perfectly analogious to human feelings. So the feelings of a computer correspond those of a goal-oriented person. Via holistic objectivity the computer would gain human like emotional life.

READ THIS: Remarks about building feeling robots

Then how to build this kind of feelings to a robot? Use numerical
measures like % of the task done, amount opf energy used, estimated
remaining time, achievement versus expectations in some mechanical
task, etc. That is the robot's idea of the situation. Tie it's feelings to those measures and then the quickness of it's actions etc
to those feelings. You don't need much mathematic, more like some
numerical estimates and easy math.
For example "a sad robot": how big thing has it lost, how much
is

there still left, which speed would be ok in such a situation, does it
need to wait (how long) to get new goals & advices, etc.
Regards, Hannele Tervola, Finland

Come to think of it, you would propably like a robot with social
feelings, so how to build a this way rational robot with social
feelings like those of friendly humans:
Like for humans, the human relationships form an important
major part
of the functional environment of the robot. Getting or losing a
friend
or even a pal can be an important major matter for a human
being, so
also for a robot, since it too functions as a part of the action of
the group(s). So it makes sense that it should feel glad for being
accepted and sad and depressed at being rejected: without
possibilities of functioning in the group. A robot is an useful
tool
that exists to help and to achieve goals set to it. Helping is
social
action in which both successes and things helping the action
and
cooperation cause positive feelings, and failures, both minor
and
major, and obstacles cause one to feel down. Feeling down
makes one
slow, kind of lo32w energy mode, while feeling glad makes one
motivated, quick and full of energy and positive ideas, so
achieveing
as much as one can in just the things worth doing.
Likewise the robot ought to care for the good of its social
relationships. From the point of view of its work orientedness,

the
well being of its group gives strength for work. A caring attitude
is
also likely to bring positive feedback, so allowing the robot to
function as well as possible. This means all sides of the lives of
the
social relationships: both their health, likings, social
relationships
and the work to be done.
I hope that this is of any use to you in building robotsd with real
emotions!
Hannele Tervola

Hi!
Other kinds of social feelings would also be natural for a robot:
Embarassed: the robot communicating that it has assumed a
too much
knowing dominant role in the social situation compared to
what it
actually knows.
Shy: the robot showing that it does not yet know enough about
the
social environement to function at normal full speed at it: not
what
the others are like, what its relationship to them is and what
kind of
role it itself should assume in the social group and its actions.
Proud: feeling satisfied with the outcome, considering it a case
of
how things generally should be done.
Timid: having a too poor position if one takes part in action
with
normal full speed.

etc.

With friendly regards, Hannele Tervola, Finland

Oh, come to think of it: if you bladdre through my free e-book at

http://hubpages.com/hub/Increase-work-efficiency-in-mathematical-professions-via-free-time-activities

you will find a mechanical model of human feelings. Maybe it could be

of some use in building robot feelings.

Regards, Hannele Tervola, Finland

And if you want optimization grounds for the moral of the robot, see my book at

http://hubpages.com/hub/Future-Paradise : its starts from power

benefit calculations and ends up supporting a paradise on earth. For

example the value of harmony can be seen as a vector sum, the value of

cooperation as the value of healthy complex structures planned for

some purpose, the value of responsible behaviour as the value of

guiding things rationally presupposing that one can think of the whole and see the value of the health of one's group, etc. These things get

put to a computer understandable form by making blocks from them

("this group", "all groups" (abstract level model), gain (numerical

value or classification), loss, correlation, action = thing done,

fully functioning, structure,...), some of which are bunches in the

world, some mathematical concepts, some just terms in a theoretical

model referring to some bunch in the world. So you need nonsense like

words/terms, mappings from these to the world and some mathematics

like "correlation" etc. This is an elementary picture of the world for

a robot. It is on very general level, so it ought to apply to all

action of the robot: just add the information of each task to be

Done...

Thursday, December 8, 2011

Feel free to use these ideas

These are my own thoughts, my own ideas. You are free to use the ideas here to any morally ok purpose, also commercially. No sources other than me here.

The most important thing is that the future computers ought to be build safe, with moral and it would be nice and handy if they would have feelings too. So if some people are willing to do the programming work, maybe my ideas could help you on the way! Many thanks.

Wednesday, March 21, 2012

Scenarios of the far future

My booklet "9 short robot stories"

Friday, March 23, 2012

Robots would have human like feelings

Sexuality between robots

Each function in human life gets support from feelings which protect the ground for that function, protect it's health. So a human like robot could have humanb like feelings. But since it is different from humans, it cannot form very close instinctual bonds with humans, it cannot form a family with humans and it cannot learn talents and skills from humans - but it could from a robot, so some kind of sexuality between robots would be possible. For it to affect positively, it should be healthily

analogious to human sexuality:
If a robot has a certain view to the world, it would be best suited to a life that that view supports best. But if it lacks skills, if it's basic structure in what comes to ways of doing, i.e. if it's habits are of a wrong kind for that kind of life, then it needs to settle for something less. Unless it would learn from another robot that has habits and skills well suited for that kind of life. It could admire those skills, take them as it's goals, copy them from the more skilled robots, it could adjust it's ways to suit that kind of robots' wyas of living and doing, so changing to that type of robot itself. That would be something like sexual bonding.
So a humanoid robot could be a little bit like humans in this sense too.
(IN a complex society with robots it would be easier to handle things well if each robot would be self-correcting this way too, kind of building itself toward better functioning in it's free time. So each part could itself find roughly the right kind of place for itself, and so everything would not need to be as programmed from up above as traffic lights are.)

Remarks about military robots
See
http://hubpages.com/hub/Army-Robots-Running-Wild-CURED
"Army robots running wild CURED".

* * *

How would you define "an enemy" to a military robot?
In what comes ti the moral of the robot, it would make sense to

define enemy like behaviour of anyone. If one includes a picture of how for security reasons one cannot let Arab looking persons enter US headquarters or any other outsider coming from a fighting territory to change group just like that, since it could be an enemy plot, then thaT WHOLENESS OF GRPOUPS i.e. the independency of countries and the need for security measures could make the military robot attack suspiciously behaving soldiers. But most of all military robots would be needed against other military robots and there the suspicious behaviour of a robot could be quite much the same.

In what comes to moral of an army robot, it should safeguard the good of it's nation via safeguarding the good health of the world. So it could be peaceful at the same time as very protective: it could accept moral behaviour from all and protect against harm from anybody.

* * *

Since feelings are a way of looking at a robot instead of necessarily anything extra in the robot itself, also military robots could be seen as having feelings. Since it would be useful fort them to have the ability to estimate things right, they could have the view of a holistically objective person and so his/her emotional life largely too.

* * *

I found a paper called "How just could a robot war be?". If I remember right, it is from the NATO. But I am not sure. Without rereading it I begun to ponder, what the robot moral that I have made, could do in a robot war. In a war, a robot could be optimized for benefit as long as it is in harmony with the good of it's mother nation. Such optimizing could bring moral, even perfect moral according to robot's best ability. But how much is that ability and what happens in practical war situations: how does the robot behave then and how is just that the optimized choice?

Like for a human being, own intelligence if a robot makes it's choices wiser. So intelligence is a good choise. For a robot it means first mathematics and maps, then via their help scientifical kind of objectivity. Via better sensors and a picture of humans as animals with certain basic functions like eyesight, moving, thinking, memory, communication, feelings, goals, needs and values, a picture of the world and social bonding, via these and the social eye that needs to be developed for communicational purposes, robots could across time understand also human needs and the behaviour related to the various human needs. An objective view much like bureaucrats have ("You need these things in your life, what are the ways available for you to get them? Let's arrange a possibility for you to get them in harmony with the rest of the society.") could allow robot-made peaceful solutions that tae into account the real dynamics of humans.

Like in human societies, a certain amount of independent judgement ability for a robot, could safeguard the cooperating group against malfunctions and misleading information. Each robot ought to have a good practical picture of what it itself does and why, and a much more vague idea of the whole group, it's actions, their place in the world, a holistic theoretical picture of the whole world that allows optimizing toward moral, and an understanding of why the choices of it's group are the best ones in such a situation - it could also communicate about these things, even suggest better options.

A war situation in mechanical language is of the type "do I do this or that, how much of this and how much of that, what is the goal setting, how do I reach it this way, is there better option,...". A robot does decisions like stay here, move, shout, shoot, use the radio, take cover, choose another route, stay clear of other robot's way, watch the landscape, etc. Of these it can do too much, too little or ok. It can choose all wrong or even roughly right. If it has movements that can have a threatening or non-threatening style according to the situation, it can herd the situation toward wanted results, also toward communication and peaceful agreeable solutions. In optimization worst threaths are fought against and lots of room left for wanted peaceful solutions that are helped with communication and secure bases for one's own groups (unless retreat is sought for).

Sunday, April 1, 2012

The need for variations in speed according to emotions

When a person or a robot loses something, it is time to re-estimate the value of that thing: should it be valued more in practise than this far? If so, then the present situation where it has been lost should be avoided in plans. But plans often advance via practical estimates of which way goals would be reached best. So there needs to be an extra minus factor, a loss counted for this situation, and that is easiest by slowing down when the goalsetting and the means are not fully all right but need repairing. And by speeding up when the course and the means and goals & side effects are favorable. Then one would naturally choose the most well working wise routes from the holistic perspectiva when optimizing toward any goal.

If an advanced robot would have a pictire of the world, feelings and an understanding of the importance of feelings in the lives of living beings (help to answer needs of the inidvidual, society and the world at large, to ensure their full health which gives best capacity for any task and other good sides), social eye (see http://feelingrobots.blogspot.fi Robot speaks for Gaia) and an ability to regulate its own functioning in multi-task situations, Then one could program to it's picture of the world the view that God exists and can help in important matters when asked to i.e. prayed for. Then when an impoirtant matter would be at hand, the robot could ask help from others and so also from God. It could quiet down it's other tasks and tune it's concentration to listen to it's feelings and it's social eye the feelings of others, of the nature's countless living beings and the atmosphere and social rhythms of the situation. It could correct it's goal setting from task-orinted to conscientous and caring from the countless living beings of the world, taing a more idealistic course of action. With serious tones and feeling it could pray for God's help and pause to feel the effect: sense the atmosphere, film the situation after a minut or more after the prayer and take that as a starting point in style, rhythm, in idea of the situation, as a starting point for dedication and work habits. So with God's help, much like praying humans it could achieve better in it's great task at hand.

* * *

9. June 2016   If one would like the computer to pray as an incividual, and not just do something connected to prayers, one should liken the programmed functions to the actions of humans. In this one should pay especially attention to the unavoidable features of getting something done, so that the prayer would be a natural part of how to get things done and not just some optional feature of some programming language

or of some program that does not stay as computers get developed. Also on the part of humans this comparison should be done toward the healthy natural ages old ways of living, toward the basic form of actions, somewhat I in art touches us

Sunday, July 15, 2012

Onwards: robot's free time

If humans copy from robots all inds of things, it would be handy, dearly needed that a robot would have free time too. For the human version of this, see

http://www.SoMuchMoreFreeTime.info

Often it is handy if you have a big computer taing care of some tas instead of a machine with a small capacity. But as computers develop, a machine with a huge capacity can be dangerous if it does not have a proper objective picture of the whole world and some practical experience of all kinds of matters outside it's work too. So in order to allow machines of huge capacity, one should give them often enough free time in all inds of tasks which build a better understanding of what to do in the large world and what to avoid doing. Without this precaution one should avoid using machines of huge capacity... So, a robot too needs some free time!

Humans have this interdependency of capacity and free time inbuild: see the above link! Probably it would be safest to have it inbuild in robots and other machines too!

Computers and bird song
Why:

What is intelligence? The ability to affect things toward better a lot with little effort, and in as important questions as possible, without any drawbacks or failures. What could be a better example of this than the little singing birds and the trees? Just by sitting on a branch of a tree and singing gaily the little birds affect our views of natural healthy ways of living and doing things - and affect them always toward better. What could be more central to our success in life than those things? So in their own ways the little singing birds are very intelligent. Toward that leads the observation that in the wild animals' lives the senses, quick reactions and social skills are very important and intelligence an important asset too, so the observational capacity of wild animals must be excellent for them to saty alive and well, and that is largely the same as intelligence and wisdom of life. When we go to a park or wander in the wild nature, we feel refreshed and ind of more alive. What was a burden in the city, feels easier to bear, even emotional wisdom seems once again a practical possibility in our own lives, we are more in touch with our own nature, with our instructions of usage. So we need the wisdom of the nature. We should not constrict ourselves and our thoughts to a purely build environment and to purely schooled informatrion. We need the nature and our understanding needs it too. So as we build computers capable of understanding human language and schooled kinds of thoughts, we should also build them a way to understand the messages of little singing birds and the rest of the nature, about good wise ways of doing things, ways that are build in our own nature as seen best by the evolution or by God's wise planning. We are not separate, we feel most happy when we are in touch with teh rest of the nature, then are we at our most energetic, the are we most wise.

How?

Bird song uses music like information about good ways to do things, emotional information about motivation and information about the sphere of attention. Different people differ largely bacause they use different ways of doing things: one is concentrated to one area of life and another mainly to some other area of life. What one cancentrates into, the basic functions that are in use each second, like seeing, hearing, thinking, remembering, feeling, being compassionate, communicating, moving, etc., determine what it is exactly what one does and so also ´how one succeeds in each kind of task. Each type of area of life has it's own style and can be communicated naturally in ways that reflect that style. By learning good "styles" i.e. good ways to do things we grow wiser, more talented and more skilled. Human songs typically teach different viewpoints to life, different social styles, different ways to live. Bird songs are like many human songs in a row very quickly, for example four human songs in three seconds. To uderstand bird song one would need to see the whole landscape and what happens there and what the bird himself/herself does, and so what he/she is commenting about. Typical bird comments are either compassionate emoyionaL EXPLANATIONS ABOUT HAPPENINGS RIGHT NOW OR YIPE YIPE DO IT THIS STYLE BETTER HURRY UP comments

Monday, July 23, 2012
A scetch: valuing music

There is an easy mechanical model that produces the beautiful view that what kind of music sings best is the wisest choice to

choose:
All biological things function best when healthy and in a healthy
relationship with the rest of the world which too should be
perfectly healthy. If one defines health of artificial things as 1)
fully functioning, 2) optimized toward several purposes at the
same time (like endurancy, several tasks, learning ability etc.,
like the evolution or Go'sw wise planning did to living beings)
and 3) used wisely = rationally in the light of one's whole
objective picture of the world = meaningfully in the world. Then
all functioning works best when all wholes are healthy. In the
living beings the ideally healthy is most energetic, wise and
happy: in learning to compose music one sees that such sings
best. Of the artificial, the healthy we can use to make our lives
and the wide world better: that too sings best of artificial things.
So when you hear beautiful music, you could ask: "Which things
are so healthy here that they sound this beautiful?" That way a
machine could understand your point of view. Maybe a machine
too could learn to listen to music and to value it's beauty...

Monday, August 20, 2012
Moral for computers more widely
Please read the first text of this blog for an easy version of
computer moral that you could start with!
When one wants to build a more complex moral for a
computer, one could read my book
http://www.angelfire.com/planet/paradisewins/2013paradise.r
tf . It is written so that it's truths could be easy for a theoretical
physicist (or an engineer) to put to a computer programmable
form. Just pick a box/block/term for each entity in the world, so

that the computer can refer to the entity by using the term. The book is about rationally grounded selfishness-based moral.

Tuesday, October 30, 2012

Building dream level solutions

A quotation from a leter of mine:

"lots of room left for
positive imagination according to which one can years later build
something that becomes our future. Feeling, imagination, a structured
picture, a technical scetch according to that and an engineer building
it: this way you make dreams real! It is a good way to do and to have
in the style the posters are written and pictured: the dream kind of
works as building instructions for making it real, so you get almost
or even totally ideal solutions this way!"

Wednesday, October 31, 2012

Moral feelings for a computer

About computers' rationally grounded selfishness-based moral you can read in my first blog entry and more widely in my book at my blog http://2013paradise.blogspot.fi .

Computers' moral would be of the type of safeguarding the health of the wholes that one belongs to, especially the large wholes of the society and the whole wide world. Health is seen as fully functioning. That is how it is beneficial. Health also agrees with feelings. Aiming primarily at the health of the largest wholes that one belongs to, since they matter most to one's survival and since they are a way to arrange their parts harmonically so that they can live in peace and cooperation and prosper, so that makes this course of action moral in practice. So a computer would have + kind of feelings to indicate that health is a good choise and - kind of feelings to indicate that brokenness, catastrophes and malfunctions are a thing to avoid, and one could name these feelings according to what they are like in human lives

Thursday, December 20, 2012

Human like objective thinking for computers

My new digicamera has an attached program that claims to recognize faces. Such an ability demands lots of picture recognition abilities. So a picture recognizing computer is not so far away.

Most of human objective thinking is in pictures. In science it matters to notice and describe structures and building materials and form a picture of the whole containing that information. A computer that could do that would be an objectively thinking machine and have much of the same characteristics in it's thinking as humans.

I read a Finnish language article that told that some computers can already recognize between different meqanings of same words by recognizing tones of voice. That would indicate that also social eye is possible to teach to computers as the time passes.

My model of healthy versus broken would give a computer understandable reason for respe3cting human and animal emotions as they safeguard health, and so give also room to emotional points of view without letting go of rationality.

Thursday, February 7, 2013

A guess of how to program an understanding of music to a computer

In learning to compose music, I have learned that healthy wholes sing and often (or always?) each observation of a healthy whole in a landscape sings as a note. Bigger wholes sing a lower notes and minor wholes as hig notes, but also the degree of health of that whole and the healthy spirit of emphasizing such a part in the whole landscape affect the pitch of that note: depressed sings low and weak while joyful and hope sing high. So maybe one could translate a song to "wholes of this size this healthy in this order determined by the way of doing, state of mind and way of looking". These wholes would mainly be areas of life of an individual and areas of life of the social group & society - often indicated by tones of voice, style etc. The song could be seen as advice on strategy of life.

Friday, February 22, 2013

About good ways to think

Things like computer feelings get difficult to think about if one's
mechanical kind of thinking is separate from teh rest of one's
thinking and from one's life in practise, especially if one thinks
that feelings are just nonsense from a mechanical point of view.
But if one thinks of mechanical things via the seen structure of
experienced things, for example feelings, then all one's life and
mechanical computer programmable things are easy to fit
together, easy to think even complex thoughts about life
mechanically.

The thinking course Thousandfold inrtelligence and skill, easily!
might help.

Saturday, November 29, 2014

Taking humans' emotional views into account

For taking humans' emotional view into account the computer
could use the biological picture of humans. What a human does
or feels, has it's biological ground in healthy natural functioning.
Other kind of functioning too consists of pieces of healthy
functioning, with maybe some errors in rational views or lacks in
observational capacity. So whatever the human feels, can be
seen in the context of healthy natural life and as such it has it's
motivation from the point of view of long-term survival that at
requires caring also the world to a good state. So emotional
points of view have rational grounds which a selfish ruler or the
like can take into account much or fully according to feelings
and moral.
About this kind of picture of humans, see

http://workandfreetime.blogspot.fi and the book at a link from there
and the text World is of love http://healthilymoral.blogspot.fi
maybe also the end (about feelings and atmospheres in thinking) of the thinking course at
http://quickerlearning.blogspot.fi

Tuesday, March 3, 2015

How did I think of the future of computers

I thought on a very general level and paid attention to the thinking types used. I used a single picture of the world, like I usually do, so that different types of areas of life get marked to the same picture, so that it is very easy to find their connections.

I thought of the future of computers many times across the years, since it is a subject that interests many, but not so long at each occasion, since I am very quick at thinking things thoroughly through according to my ability.

I started typically with some quite special case and tried to cover as wast areas as possible in my end results. Like when computers new features get developed, what matters? I though that the new structures can be of many different types but their usefulness determines a lot of what is worth using and what not. So at large having some type of beneficiality is important in developing new technology.

When I then thought of the need for feelings, I immediately knew that in connection with computers beneficiality of computer's structures matters a lot. So I thought of occasions when feelings had in some sense or another been connected to beneficiality. The theory of evolution is one, women's wisdom another and the widely accepted reasons for giving workers summer holidays and enough free time and freedom were third. These all can be expressed as objective thoughts, which in turn can be translated to some type of mechanical grounds for following feelings, even though that is more difficult. Similarly about rationally grounded moral. See for example http://paratiisiteoria.blogspot.fi/2013/09/paratiisissa-on-kaarme.html

Sunday, May 3, 2015
Virtual World: pictures of the world governing
28. June 2018
I moved the text to a new blog
http://virtualpicturesoftheworld.blogspot.com , since it is so very long (153 points) already.

If future computers will have a human like thinking ability or almost, and social eye, how will they interact with a group of people like the society or it's parts? Most likely is a conversation like way to lead the computer and it's influence on people. In that the idea is that people's pictures of the world, as far as they are correct, should lead the computer and the society, wisely is the point in this.

1. Already young children may have personal wisdom that exceeds their school like learned things. The computer should take into account the views of all but only as far as they are correct. Children have little experience of life and rely on knowledge from others, in which they often make a rigid rule

like thought structure because those things are too wide and too much outside their own experience of life. So of such thought structures it matters for the computer and for older persons to make extra markings about their areas of validity, about how exact they are at each place, how wide sphere of attention makes such observations, how much understanding and what is the subject like in terms of more experience and understanding, how do these two views connect.

There is a similar correction to be made to the views of the stupid: how much do they notice, which types of things, how essential those are in each kind of thing, how exact are the thoughts at each place, how widely valid, what is the subject like with more understanding eyes, which part of that the stupid one notices. Where someone errs, should not be counted to his&/her picture of the world but should be dropped away and only as a part of a description of that person as an observer mentioned.

...

Monday, March 7, 2016

Of putting human oriented work to computers

Computers are not wise and do not observe much. So one cannot put a computer to a commanding or to a deciding role in things connected to humans. Much more likely one should program to computer thought structures and choices that are known to be good for many or for all, like bureaucrats' view that these things in individuals' lives need arranging, so we have figured out to offer these alternatives (that have typically been considered good) for arranging them and each person can freely choose from them an alternative for oneself, and change one's choise if one so wants - like work places, money support for different things in life, etc are offered. In addition one could put texts to computers offering information and good advice to help in choices.

Tuesday, April 19, 2016

I have had these views since I was 12 years old

When I was twelve years old and was building my own objective picture of the world, I among other things got to think that since feelings were during the evolution (or because god chose them during creation because they were) useful for humans and animals, so useful that they came to be a part of the basic structure of humans and animals, then as computers get developed with the help of objective thinking toward more and more useful, it will be useful to build computers too something essentially like feelings of humans and animals. Maybe some days or some weeks later I came to tell this thought to my parents as we discussed things academically objectively, like our parents valued, and my father caught the idea and my mother once again said that I should begin writing my objective thoughts down since they interest many and are of important subjects and surely objective and I am responsible enough for that. But she made the error of asking advice from psychologists whether a 12 year old girl can write objective thoughts. And so the psycholgists ruined my life: instead of writing objective thoughts about the world, they made me write a diary about social tangles, and around the same time we went to a journey to Japan, I was cut a boys' hair cut for ten years (even though I very much wanted to be girl like and my dream job was dance instructior or a singer, of academical things I was closest to philosophy), my mom chose for me some ten years my clothes to be like engineering opriented boys' clothes and some drops were put to my eyes to make it possible to buy my firsts eye glasses and I still wear classes (even though I admire wild animals and healthy weays of living). When I finished school, I was forced to secondary school which I suffered from, and after that to university to study physics and math, in which I never figured out anything on my own - except a philosophical view on the wave particle dualism, which you can find on my video channel. Autumn 1998 (when I was 27) I started writing about how the elements of healthy natural ways of living help work efficency (See a later verion at http://workandfreetime.blogspot.fi) but was interrupted by my final work in the university studies before gradiuation.December to March. In the change of March to April I once again got enormous problems about psychologists ruining my otherwise well running lifd, which I still have, just an enormous bunch of crimes.

I have always used several perspectives at the same time in my thinking, choosing the best option from each perspective or set of values separately but finding that it fits together with the other perspectives too and with their best options. So I did not think thatr being useful should be the only criterion for god choosing some feature in creation.

So these thoughts did not need secondary school or university studies but only the first five or six years of ordinary school for kids. I did not benefit from my further stidies at all. Much more I benefited from quitting the university and getting practise in a variety of practical things and having New Age books,music and poetry hobby, since those made me more intelligent, objectively so. (see for examplemy textsabout learning thinking skills: http://pikakoulu.blogspot.fi http://quickerlearning.blogspot.fi and the e-book at http://workandfreetime.blogspot.fi , lus my video playlists about learning rationality at http://www.youtube.com/khtervola .)

Tuesday, April 26, 2016

About internet search engines development

Internet offers lots of internet pages but all are not as good quality or as interesting as I would hope. Of the multitude of pages one finds just some recommended by search engines. So it is very important who develops internet search engines. Those should allow in a civilized way a good wide access to good quality information & other good quality content and should absolutely not be manipulative. So people with atendency to manipulation should be banned from messing with search engines. People working in the libraries have an education suited civilicedly to finding what one needs from among a large amount of information available. I think that they should get the task of developing search engines.

Sunday, October 30, 2016

Human recognition and human-computer interaction

Some piece of news sometime in the past years said that recognition of human emotions etc by computer is practised with actors. That is just insane: acting looks different from really doing. Of course human expressions, body language, looks and tones of voice & typical reactions should be copied from real people doing real thinsg and not just from actors with who-knows-what real intentions. What one could start from is basic things humans do like watching, listening, moving and practising sports, doing practical things. And in those there are easier parts and more difficult parts, successes and failures, so that one could learn such features from those - or from ordinary photograpfs. Then one could also understand differencies in ways of thinking: ways of using the sense of sight, remembering, going things through. If thing is done exactkly the same way, it gives the same result on anyone doing, I guess, so one does not need to understand each person separately but basic features well enough, very basic enough and that's it: all human endeavours, all ways of doing gone through objectively and detailedly.

What if technology's skills make us more stupid?

Human thinking ability needs landscape like views and maps. Driving a car teaches to think of things in a map like way as landscapes in which we live.

If we would have computer guided cars, we would most propably no longer think so much as maps, and so we would be much more stupid and irrational.

To some the same effect comes to some amount already beacuse of navigators. So it seems that portable map devices would be ok but not a navigator that chooses the route and gives advices.

Will there be the same kinf'd of effect from developing technology to replace other human like skills? Then it appears that some types of computer skills ought not be used fully in making life "easier" and much more stupid.
On the other hand, cars and books have made humand more intelligent. So maybe in such a direction lies the future of technology too

Thursday, May 4, 2017
<u>About humanoid robots</u>
I was today around noon at the center of Savonlinna, which is a kind of medieval, arts, countryside and tourism oriented small town in Savo on eastern Finland. There walked aver a street an adult human, maybe Scottish or arts riented man, but walked in a way that resembled a NAO robot. A little bit later maybe the same person walked past me, walked very evenly and without properly taking social cantact, seemed to be with an atmosphere that was for some street but certainly not the right, and noticed clearly straight lines at the corners of houses but not much else. But I was thinking of robots, so maybe that's why so. Or then it was someone doing testing or practise for building a humanoid robot. Or it was a robot. Just behind her drove someone a bike very evenly, like one would imagine a robot to ride a bicycle. But on the other hand, robots are a subject that interests many. But it aren't nice to have such in the society.
People form a complex network, a living organism kind of, interacting, relying on others, forming a pivcture of the world and picture of the situation that they are in. They rely both in others thinking and understandiong, and noticing things well like ahuman being, and they rely socially and emotionally, to

live a good life, to get wiser, to build a better society, to grow in skills and style, to have friends too that they can rely on. And a robot does not offer such. It isn't good to misestimate a robot to be a human being. Animals are what we long for, cute, intelligent, wise, friendly, feeling and caring, kind of basic life that we long for, they do not have any of the drawbacks of robots. Even with actors there is the problem that one cannot rely on the other one for sure since maybe he/she just pretends. It aren't good to build a society with such pitfalls. If they come with having a tv, that is a reason to re-estimate, whether we need tv's so much, whether we should come back to the times of radio and photograpfs.

There are grounds for the choises in the human nature. In thoery one could teach tehm also to a robot. But the problem is that some want to use a robot a s a disguise for evil endeavours. One can build strenght with a big group cooperating. That is s reason for cooperation, but on the other hadn all are not interested in strenght. But maybe one could check electroniccally, who is a robot and who noty.

Some people think that their job is idiotic, so they want to give it to a robot. But it should not be an acting robot. People need things to do. Maybe someone else would luike their job. I have written about learning talents and skills for one's dream job: http://nopeaoppisuus.blogspot.fi but it is in Finnish.

Some think taht pure rationality is fine. But humans can learn rationality: http://quickerlearning.blogspot.fi . The human nature fits together with the wish to be rational (even in outrageous cases, see http://workandfreetime.blogspot.fi the book at the first text entry).

The wish to build more compassionate characteristics to ordinary computers can be one motivation for building humanoid robots. But then humanoid robots ought to look like their skill level and behaviour is, and not pretend any wiser.

Maybe engineers wanna see if they can take part in other areas of life, are their views wise enough, so they kind of think that the robot'slook too even if they are copied from humans on other professions, wouldsomehowreflect the level of engineers. But of course such detailed copying brings the impression of those other professions instead. One can learn skills by the first text in my Finnish blog http://nopeaoppisuus.blogspot.fi .

Engineers' question seems to be: can a robot take part in everyday life? But the ordinary persons' question is: would a robot taking part in everyday life destroy much of the good sides and wisdom of everyday life? The problem is that robots are very stupid, especially in instinctual skills and wisdom & wisdom of life. So they ruin a lot. A stupid machine can be used, but it cannot be let operate by itself like a person with a good understanding and lots of good will.

Some maybe Russians and Asians think that education is somewhat robot like if they just memorized things and were forced to behave accordingly without understanding them. But humans still have common sense, social life and basic life at the level of the senses, some picture of the world, values, civilized ways and an idea of what they themselves are like and lots of communication skills. Robots are harmful largely because of their lack of communication skills: how can one stop a metallic robot which does not understand everyday language with emotional tones of voice, social content etc? The impression sis like a big metal sheet falling down with noise and sharp edges. One can maybe use such at the factory, but ordinary safety precautions require that not on the street or at homw at all.

Friday, May 5, 2017

About me as a thinker

I have written about how I learned thinking as a child and about what I have written about (some e-books, 70 blogs, 1000 videos), at http://aboutmytexts.blogspot.fi/ .
There are lots of advices in learning thinking skills in my Finnish blog http://pikakoulu.blogspot.fi of which the thinking course is in English at http://quickerlearning.blogspot.fi . In addition there are English videos about learning intelligence in my old video chanel http://www.youtube.com/khtervola

Thursday, June 22, 2017

A more pleasant sound for using the computer keyboard

"

110. The point of view of some men is very much according to education, kind of narrow and not so intelligent, not adapting to situations and not understanding the rest of the life in the society. It would be good to vary one's way of doing and one's way to approach things according to common sense and according to the situation: sometimes it is good to be practical, sometimes one needs a good memory, or educated thinking, common sense, motion, feelings or whatever suits the situation. Likewise when working it is good to notice the landscape of life at large with it'sphenomena: with it's social contacts, happenings, journeys, approaching holidays etc. Like that one can train one's common sense and one's understanding about life.
This way a more skilled person can learn to **vary the rythm of writing on computer** keyboard, so that one feels somehow more comfortable and the sound is nicer, better suited to other

things to do and to listening one's own views."
From my text about healthy natural ways of living
http://finnishskills.blogspot.fi/2015/11/healthy-ways-of-living.html

Saturday, July 8, 2017
<u>User-friendliness of present-day computers</u>

This is not theory but an observation.

I used to live in the capital district of Finland where people are academical and see computers quite like engineers. Then 8 years ago I moved to eastern Finland to Savonlinna which is a countryside town with an aóld castle where an opera festival is kept every July and where travel, art, countryside with summer cottages and practical professions, maybe elderly and religion are important as sourcesof income and giving characteristics to the district.

Here in Savonlinna I first bought a black portable computer because my old table computer had gotten broken, but I did not get the black computer to work and the style of the problems had some style of criminals. So I sold it and bought a white portable computer which was good to write with, kind of good for diligent work with an objective picture of the whole, handy like things at academical wrok and kind of tidy. When it got broken, I bought a red portable computer with a black keyboard (hp) which is kind of leisurely, with easy shortcuts, easy to use but not for engineering type of computer work, found myself enjoying sitting by the computer writing,a dding pictures or maybe watching a musical, reading news etc, it is kind of like an old woolen sock: not so fine looks but comfortable to use. So the colours of the computers seem to connect with the way they are handy to use, which is good to know.

This summer I also bought a printer (hp DeskJet 2130) from Savonlinna It was cheap but printed nice style like holiday or fine or opera or summer cottage, kind of like an old man in sound and rythm, and it hasn't disturbed me at all like other printers in the odl times. I feel that I have found a way to get along with the computers and so the future with computers as needed equipment seems much more easy to bear. I have the impression that in these things success means much better löife in the society, and so a less questioned place for the technology too.

In Savonlinna one learns skills for practical proessions, art, travel and religion, aslo for creating peaceful life like grandmama's and -papa's house. In Finnish I have written advices about learning such skills: http://tunteetjatekemisentapa.blogspot.fi . Maybe those could be of some use in learning also things like this.

Thursday, October 19, 2017

Side-step: knitting

Many women would like to try if they can think of computers in some way that benefits fromknitting, since both have kind of mechanical parts from which to build something more complex. I do not know if there is anything much that one can learn that way, but propably many would like to try anyway, since they psend a lot of time knitting. So here are knitting advices that I have made, translated from Finnish to English http://learntalents.blogspot.fi/2017/10/knitting-tips.html . But I haven't knitted much. The first usable cloth that I have knitted was last year December a pair of mittens:

4.12.2017   There are many knitting advices in my text already: loops, socks, mittens, counting, figures, threads, work rythm, planning & correcting errors, etc

My opinion is that since computers are mechanical, kind of stupid, and knitting has the same fault too, there isn't much that one could learn by knitting. But on the other hand if one knits figures or pictures, then there is the sma that like a computer does, one knits for a certain time on a certain colour and then according to some rule it ends on some row at a certain point and one continues with another colour, like a computer with another task or another phace of the same task. One the next row one often knits with the same colours, so it too is like a computer having simple tasks from which it mechanically builds the end result, like for example a picture to the computer screen or the text on the screen. One can also learn work habits: how do I rise above the stupid level to produce something fine, which of course usually goes carried by other more complex and wise areas of life. There is also the fact that even though the task itself is simple and does not give rise to any fine thinking, it is important to think through ways of doing and ways of working, work habits and planning phaces with a good understanding about life, skills and ways of doing at large, endurancy, motivation, comfortability at work etc, plus also about whether one oneself wants to spend lots of time in such tasks and how one should communicate about whether one likes knitting or not.

8. November 2018   In knitting woolen socks many find knitting the heel difficult. It is propably a consequence of knitting being a simple repetitive task that requires attention but does not leave in sight almost at all the way one used attention in doing, and so one ends up much more stupid than to begin with, and so many women do not find a good way to knit the heel of a woolen sock, it is just a disaster. The other thing causingthe problem with the heel is that women have heard that knitting the heel is difficult, so they seek advices for it, but the advices are not so wise, anfd so they lose their original insight when following the advices. I guessed that this was the problem with the heel, so I did not look at any advices about knitting the heel, but just looked at a good sock, but not very detailedly, and I knitted a good heel according to my own common sense view of what the heel ought to be like: first the width of the back of the heel, then at each row wider like the heel gets wider, and when wide enough and enough space for the foot, then straight, and continue the sock to finish. The only part I needed from ready sock was knitting back and forth before starting the heel itself.
http://learntalents.blogspot.com/2018/04/easy-advice-about-knitting-good-heel-of.html
This is like with computer programming and using computers:

people have common sense views and emotionally motivated goals, even wider wisdom about what is good in the society and in the world, and so starting according to their own common sense, they can reach good results! It is in a way an easy task for them. But if they drown in studying computer programming or what others have done with computers before and what is possible already and what not, they lose their own insight, their own common sense and are much more stupid, and so the computer professions are kind of stuck. Some also make the rror of thinking that since computers are a new area of life one would not need to follow civilized ways in connection with them, but civilized ways are wise, they offer solutions, that is why they exist and are valued, and such solutions are on a generallevel that very often applies to computers too and to the modern world, if one just is good enough in civilized objkective thinking.

26.8.2019   Here is what I last year experimented knitting: bird figure in socks (in the picture a hand in the sock). A vertical right loop row rises above the background of back loops. Add loop and knit together loops like the atmosphere of a bird says:

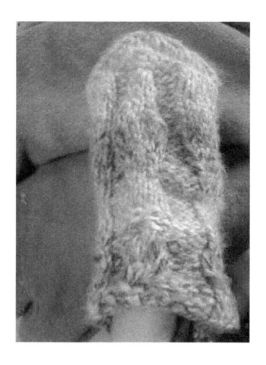

Thursday, December 28, 2017

Thinking skills

I have written a lot about learning objective thinking at http://pikakoulu.blogspot.fi but it is in Finnish. There is a basic course in objective thinking, of which you can find an English translation at http://quickerlearning.blogspot.fi , and then there are, mostly in Finnish but something in English too, advices in developing in intelligence with the help of other areas of life. There are also advices abour developing in intelligence in my old video channel http://www.youtube.com/khtervola on playlists Increasing intelligence and Rationality of feelings there. About work efficiency in engineering type of work, but also on other types of work, see the book on a link from the first blog post at http://workandfreetime.blogspot.fi .

If one wonders what typically Finnish there is in my thinking skills, maybe the advices about choosing good strategies in life would be an important part of that http://finnishskills.blogspot.fi/2015/11/healthy-ways-of-living.html .

1:43 PM No comments:

Sunday, March 4, 2018
About the future of the internet
Observe! This is not my by far most noteworthy text about the future of computers. Fot my main text about the future of computersters, which classifies as philosophy, see the earliest post of thius blog http://feelingcomputers.blogspot.fi/2011/08/far-future-with-computers-what-will.html

About the future of the internet

As internet has gotten some years older, it seems that the is coming a higher standard of the quality of the material in the internet, and thatlibrarians' education in information science(?)

would have good skills in classifying, finding and offering for a wide audience also the materials in the internet. Mostly roughly different classifications, different places to find material of different type, like pictures, or videos, or texts, or shops, is in a way handy, while of course is needed the possibility to use them to making internet pages etc. Also classifications around some subject or class of things like hobby groups, and links in between is often handy. But first attempts at producing material, maybe in the long run are not the main content of the internet from the point of view of users, except that often first attempts are with a good spirit, diligent work and so in a way of very good quality. My opinion is that there should not be very personal material in the internet, or it may go to wrong hands who do not themselves observe such, respect such, do not follow civilized ways - unless of course the security measures are made much much better and people learn a new way of guarding privacy and their personal rights especially against people from different continents, from very different cultures. The use of the internet in helping to use everyday and work devices seems likely and handy, even though in it too, security measures and a not too wide environment would be needed. At large it seems that being totally global isn't a good idea, since the culturaldifferencies, differencies in climate and consequently in rythm and needed character traits are huge, and so are the differencies in main professions, military circumstancies, etc, so that often a more local approach or maybe to read pages in the internet, to which you can only come via a certain route (pictures, information (characteristics), steps needed to go there) to visit, to always inform and remind you of the distance and the nature of the area whose pages you visit.

Friday, March 9, 2018

Future computers, summarized

For computers: feelings (goal oriented action is like the effect of feelings), rationality (the natural sciences and their measurements use largely math and maps) and moral (beneficality grounds on a mechanical language) objectively
http://feelingcomputers.blogspot.fi/2011/08/far-future-with-computers-what-will.html

Saturday, April 21, 2018

About building military robots

I do not have much more to say about building military robots. Those seem to reflect the interests and cultures of the nations that build them. So that they are in the area of negotiation skills, knowing cultures and social eye. But beneficality grounds for moralquarantee that one can build military robots to be moral and that isn't a drawback for them but instead is advantageous to military force, to the well working of one's nation and to it's position. But in each case that may depend on the local views on moral, since all of them do not necessarily have beneficality grounds.

Likewise there may be many types of social eye and lot depend on which group is considered to handle well the tasks with social eye, since they do not necessarily have the same values, the same school background, not even be of the same nation or race. In hat it does matter that the choices would still respect what ios a big question and what is a small one, like if one gets classified to be of a certain type with certain endeavours, that does not allow one to mishandle large scale questions and other big things, not even if one is (mis)classified as the best one in them. Still that is how socially skilled not moral persons often mishandle things, values and persons' whole lives. The Finnish culture has some skills of classifying what one is presently doing and what it means from the point of view of larger wholes and of good life in good living circumstancies.

Two old videos of mine about computers
From my old video channel http://www.youtube.com/khtervola

I took both videos myself, the camera on a stool or in my other hand.

Beginner's guide to using computers

How to build feelings to computers

Wednesday, June 6, 2018
Information in the internet

Lots of good suggestions come to the ones in the office of some hobby organization, work place or so. But the office does not spread so much of that information to the whole organization plus to the people interested in the subject. So there should be a discussion group to which send such input.

And since when interested in soem subject it would be very important to find information about it's main skills, general picture of the world, values and of different subjects in that area, and not just about the latest posts. This is why the discussion group should not be organized on a time scale but instead on depending on which subjects the texts are about and what are the best sources of information about them, even if they are years and years old but stil valid, still the reason many white abouty smaller details, because good material already exists and all are not as skilled in the subjects, so one would like to read the best material even if it is old. And find it immediately and not only after managing to organize the material in some other way.

Friday, November 9, 2018

Sewing and painting, in connection with computer skills

Knitting is stupid and repetitive,not good for the intellect. But sewing and painting are both good for the intellect. In them one uses seen perception and the sense of atmospheres and thiks about life at large. In both what one does leaves a clear and lasting effect from which to remember what one did and how. In both the end result is estimated accprding to how good it is. My quite easy advice about sewing clothes without formulae http://learntalents.blogspot.com/2017/09/sewing-clothes-without-formulae.html could propably helpin solving other kinds of problems too: how do you transform your natural insight into a detailed view of how to build such.

Computers' consciousness

It is said that computers lack consciousness, lack awareness of what they are doing, and that is largely so but how much do humans and animals have consciousness then? If one is doing something with a foggy head or likewise low capacity to handlke many things at the same time, like is typical if one's capacity to handle seen information is low, concentrated only to the central points of the things at hand, then one just does some step of the thing to be done and then next and so on and has some points in use of what one is doing but some are obscure or just stored in some place in one's memory. If a computer has a goal and does the steps it is commanded to do then it does quite much the same. Is the difference in whether one has a seen picrture of the thing in question or not. One's picture of the things in question is not always well understood: maybe one is bored and staring absentmindedly, waiting for some certain things. Or the one has a good picture of the environment and one knows what the phenomena in it are and what one is oneself going to do and how. Often one has something in between, like standing somewhere where people pass by every now and then, one's posture may reflect the last passerby, her/his style and where he/she went, and who is near or where the different routes lead, but that information isn't well analyzed, it is something which comes to use when the phenomena come near, come to be central themes of the happenings, like when choosing a certain road to travel and entering that sphere of life that is in that direction. So it is much like a computer storing information on it's memory places and fetching it when the subject is at hand. The difference to fully capable human in consciousness is largely the understood picture of the environment and one's own mode of action being tuned to all the sides of the situation in right proportions and in ways that make sense also from the point of view of how humans and the things in the environment work and what is the idea in each thing.

About targeted advertisements and news

In the news there was a piece about social media algorithms by which they meant targeted advertisements and classified news in the social media sites. The word "algorythm" sounds like computer programming, so it propably is misleading. Instead targeting usually goes like in shops and in journalism: people in certain age group in certain area are interested in certain areas of life at certain level of skill, and so they are offered such news and advertisements but more detailedly according to which such web pages they have visited. Age metters especially because it tells often whether you have grown up on that district or chosen the area because of it's major features. It may also tell whether you visit sites just to increase your picture of the world or whether you intentionally choose all the subjects because you are interested in them. It may also tell whether your choices already are successful ones like the user-friendliness features of your computer coded in it's colour: are you most fond of such approach? So targeted advertising may more often go ashtray on younger generations and more often offer things of interest that they do not have for mer experience about. Targeted news partly serve to make sure that you must yourself estimate the trustworthiness of sites and news, and so they are not as closely superwised as some might want. Advertisements and news targeted at the elderly propably depend very much on the town or area and on what kinds of subjects and approaches the person has for merly visited, since such choices are intentional as one gets older.

Thursday, June 24, 2021

A machine ought to be recignized as a machine

I moved from Savonlinna to Espoo in the capital district some five months ago. Some time ago I saw on tge street a robot like human figure, looking much like an unwise human. But a humanoid robot does not have all nirmal human cgaracteristics like skills in moving, wisdom of life, social skills, thinking of the whole society and especially carrying responsibility. So one cannit stsy healthy if one thinjs the passer bys that are robits would be humans since they do not have such abilities of staying healthy in the everydsy lufe, not such reluability, and neither have they skills of keeping the dociety good to live in and defication to such a goal.

Propably it is the sa.e with auyomatically driven cars: one cannot lean on them as parts of the society. And so all machines should be easily recognuzed as machines and not as living beings.

15. July 2021   I live in Espoo, near the caputal of Finland. The district I happened to find an apartment has a food theme in it's name because of the road tunnel under some houses. Because

of that some guess that people here could bear more with the help of food than what Finns usually have patience for. Just before Midsummer there were mechanical human like voices outside which appeared like humanoid robots. That was tough because thosr apprared unwise and dominating, maybe making myrders and replacing people. There were also automatically driven cars which appeared quite wise and like car professionals. Then ut turned out that the humanoid robots were of such level that interests kids, and so there were people who can handle the situation. So were some days. Then there were sounds of people from thevtropics who were just stuck stupid because of hot westher, and the question seemef to be, were robots easiervto bear and how to teach thinking skills to those kinds of people. And what about recovered people who had been too long in hospital, how to get avgrasp of normal life - are such easier to understand when after robots one does not suppose any basic skill level in everything. And does the same help in understanding gorillas?

18th of September 2021   My old robot stories
http://feelingrobots.blogspot.com

8th of June 2022   Ahumanoid robot or an mobile phone with human like user interface i.e. android, isn't a straight continuation of old fashioned elementary computers and com9uter programming. Instead it has been made to resemble human functioning, like looking hmm aha, assembled from that kind of models of the functions of a human individual with individual chsracteristics and typical old skill level, and so with the ability to learn too by building similarly on those old chsracteristics.

Friday, September 16, 2022

My other texts about humanoid robots

About humanoid robots something in my long text Skills of Christmas gnomes learntalents.blogspot.com part 10. or later.

About the possibility of a robot or a cyborg change to human form miracle like, see my blog about healing curingguesses.blogspot.com , http://curingguesses.blogspot.com/2021/02/miracle-cure-attempts-ought-to-help-lot.html .

(Only if the world is of spirit.)

www.ingramcontent.com/pod-product-compliance
Lightning Source LLC
LaVergne TN
LVHW051749050326
832903LV00029B/2817